Beyond Redress: Prioritising the Child's Best Interests to Achieve Equality before the Law in South Africa

Using the Best Interests of the Child to Challenge Race and Gender Discrimination

By Salatiso

For Sazi

Copyright

salatiso@salatiso.com

Dedication

To & for Sazi,
Always.

iSazisi

1. Every child has the right—
    a. to a name and a nationality from birth;
    b. to family care or parental care, or to appropriate alternative care when removed from the family environment;
    c. to basic nutrition, shelter, basic health care services and social services;
    d. to be protected from maltreatment, neglect, abuse or degradation;
    e. to be protected from exploitative labour practices;
    f. not to be required or permitted to perform work or provide services that—
        i. are inappropriate for a person of that child's age; or
        ii. place at risk the child's well-being, education, physical or mental health or spiritual, moral or social development;
    g. not to be detained except as a measure of last resort, in which case, in addition to the rights a child enjoys under sections 12 and 35, the child may be detained only for the shortest appropriate period of time, and has the right to be—
        i. kept separately from detained persons over the age of 18 years; and
        ii. treated in a manner, and kept in conditions, that take account of the child's age;
    h. to have a legal practitioner assigned to the

child by the state, and at state expense, in civil proceedings affecting the child, if substantial injustice would otherwise result; and

i. not to be used directly in armed conflict, and to be protected in times of armed

j. conflict.

2. **A child's best interests are of paramount importance in every matter concerning the child.**

3. In this section "child" means a person under the age of 18 years.

Section 28, Children, SA Constitution, Bill of Rights

1. Everyone is equal before the law and has the right to equal protection and benefit of the law.
2. Equality includes the full and equal enjoyment of all rights and freedoms. **To promote the achievement of equality, legislative and other measures designed to protect or advance persons, or categories of persons, disadvantaged by unfair discrimination may be taken.**
3. The state may not unfairly discriminate directly or indirectly against anyone on one or more grounds, including race, gender, sex, pregnancy, marital status, ethnic or social origin, colour, sexual orientation, age, disability, religion, conscience, belief, culture, language and birth.
4. No person may unfairly discriminate directly or indirectly against anyone on one or more grounds in terms of subsection. National legislation must be enacted to prevent or prohibit unfair discrimination.
5. Discrimination on one or more of the grounds listed in subsection (3) is unfair unless it is established that the discrimination is fair.

Section 9, Equality, SA Constitution, Bill of Rights

Preface: The Child's Compass Points the Way

In the heart of South Africa, a nation grappling with its complex past and the aspirations for its future, lies a principle with the power to transform the lives of its most vulnerable citizens: the best interests of the child. Enshrined in Section 28 of the South African Constitution, this principle should serve as a guiding light for all decisions and actions concerning children. Yet, three decades after the fall of apartheid, the promise of a "rainbow nation" built on equality and justice remains unfulfilled.

Well-intentioned redress policies have inadvertently created new challenges. State-sanctioned discrimination, even under the guise of "fair discrimination," has perpetuated inequality and exacerbated social ills. The "born-frees," who should have inherited a nation of equal opportunity, now face a country with more race and gender-based legislation than during apartheid, as reported by AfriForum. This generation, and their children, grapple with the consequences: failed public services, soaring unemployment rates, rampant crime, and a society plagued by numerous social issues.

This book argues that there is no policy decision that does not ultimately impact children. Whether it's employment equity legislation, economic policy, or social welfare programs, every decision reverberates through society and affects the lives of children. For instance, employment policies that discriminate against certain groups directly impact a parent's ability to provide for their children. Economic policies that disproportionately allocate funding affect the resources available for children's education, health, and well-being.

Section 28 of the Constitution asserts that a child's best interests are of paramount importance in every matter concerning the child. This book contends that every policy in the country ultimately concerns children, and as such, every policy decision should be subject to this provision. By adopting this perspective, we can create a society where every child is valued, protected, and empowered, regardless of their race, gender, or socioeconomic background.

The journey ahead is challenging. South Africa's history of apartheid and ongoing struggles with inequality have created deep-seated biases and systemic barriers that continue to affect children's lives. However, the best interests of the child principle provides a powerful framework for challenging these injustices and advocating for change.

This book is a call to action for all South Africans. It is for parents, caregivers, educators, social workers, activists, and anyone who believes in the power of the law to create a more just and equitable society. By understanding the best interests of the child principle and its potential to transform our nation, we can work together to build a brighter future for all.

In advocating for the superiority of the best interests of the child principle over redress provisions, this book emphasises the far-reaching impact of policy decisions on children. It argues that when state-sanctioned discrimination disadvantages a parent, it inherently disadvantages the child as well. From economic stability to access to opportunities, every policy decision shapes the environment in which children grow and develop.

By placing the best interests of the child at the forefront of all policy and legal decisions, we can build a society that truly values and invests in its future generations. This requires addressing the root causes of inequality, challenging discriminatory practices, and advocating for policies that prioritise the well-being of all children, regardless of their background.

As we embark on this exploration, we must ask ourselves:

- Can the best interests of the child principle serve as a powerful tool to challenge and dismantle state-sanctioned discrimination?

- Can it be a compass that guides us towards a future where all children have the opportunity to thrive and reach their full potential?

This book argues that the answer is a resounding yes, and invites all South Africans to join in the effort to create a more just and equitable society for our children and generations to come.

Part I: Historical Evolution of the Best Interests Principle

1. Ancient and Medieval Origins of Child Welfare

In our quest to understand the best interests of the child principle and its potential to reshape South African society, we must first journey back through time to explore the earliest conceptions of child welfare. This chapter examines how ancient civilizations and mediaeval societies approached the care and protection of children, laying the groundwork for modern child rights principles.

1.1. Early Conceptions of Child Welfare in Ancient Civilizations

While the concept of childhood as a distinct stage of life with inherent rights is a relatively modern development, ancient civilizations did recognize the importance of protecting and nurturing children. In many societies, children were viewed as blessings from the gods or ancestral spirits, and their well-being was seen as essential for the continuation of the family lineage and the prosperity of the community.

In ancient Egypt, for example, children were cherished and protected by law. The goddess Isis was revered as the divine mother and protector of children, and her image was often depicted in amulets and other objects associated with childbirth and child-rearing. The ancient Egyptians also had laws that prohibited infanticide and child abuse, and they recognized the importance of education and training for children.

In ancient Mesopotamia, the Code of Hammurabi, one of the earliest known legal codes, included provisions for the care and upbringing of children. The code emphasised the responsibility of parents to provide for their offspring and outlined punishments for those who neglected or abused children.

In ancient Greece and Rome, philosophers and legal scholars recognized the importance of nurturing and educating children for the betterment of society. Plato, in his Republic, advocated for the education of both boys and girls, while Aristotle emphasised the importance of early childhood experiences in shaping an individual's character and potential.

In ancient China, Confucian philosophy emphasised filial piety, the respect and obedience owed to one's parents and ancestors. This principle extended to the care and upbringing of children, who were seen as the future of the family and society. Confucian teachings also stressed the importance of education and moral cultivation for children, emphasising the role of parents and teachers in shaping their character and values.

1.2. Mediaeval Developments in Child Welfare

The mediaeval period witnessed a complex interplay of religious, cultural, and legal influences on the understanding of child welfare. The rise of Christianity brought a renewed emphasis on the sanctity of life and the importance of protecting the vulnerable, including children. Religious institutions played a significant role in providing care and education for orphans and abandoned children, establishing a precedent for the state's responsibility in child protection.

In Europe, the mediaeval church established orphanages and foundling hospitals to care for abandoned children. These institutions, while often overcrowded and underfunded, provided a vital safety net for children who would otherwise have been left to fend for themselves. The church also played a role in regulating marriage and family life, emphasising the importance of parental responsibility for the care and upbringing of children.

In the Islamic world, the Quran and the teachings of the Prophet Muhammad emphasised the importance of compassion and kindness towards children. Islamic law provided detailed guidelines for the care and upbringing of children, including their rights to inheritance, education, and protection from harm.

In Africa, traditional societies had their own approaches to child welfare, often rooted in communal values and practices. Children were seen as belonging to the community as a whole, and their upbringing was a shared responsibility. Elders played a crucial role in transmitting cultural knowledge and values to children, while the community as a whole provided support and protection.

1.3. The Xhosa Tradition of Child-Rearing: A Communal Tapestry of Nurturing and Resilience

The Xhosa people of southern Africa, like many other African cultures, have a rich tradition of child-rearing that emphasizes the importance of family, community, and cultural identity. Children are seen as gifts from the ancestors and are cherished and nurtured by their families and the wider community.

In traditional Xhosa society, child-rearing was a collective responsibility, with grandparents, aunts, uncles, and other relatives playing an active role in the upbringing of children. As I explored in my book, *The Homeschooling Father*, this communal approach was not only a cultural norm but a practical necessity in a society where resources were often scarce and families relied on each other for support. This shared responsibility fostered a strong sense of belonging and identity, as children learned their cultural traditions, values, and beliefs from multiple sources within their extended family and community.

The Xhosa also have specific rituals and practices that mark important milestones in a child's life, such as birth, naming ceremonies, initiation rites, and marriage. These rituals serve to reinforce the child's connection to their family, community, and ancestors, and to prepare them for their roles and responsibilities as adults. For instance, the *imbeleko* (welcoming ceremony for a newborn) celebrates the arrival of a new life and integrates the child into the community. Initiation rites like *ulwaluko* (circumcision for boys) and *intonjane* (initiation for girls) mark the transition to adulthood and impart important cultural knowledge and values.

These traditional practices, deeply rooted in the principles of *ubuntu* (interconnectedness and shared humanity), offer a holistic approach to child-rearing that prioritises the well-being and development of the child within the context of their family and community. This approach aligns with the best interests of the child principle, which emphasises the importance of considering the child's physical, emotional, psychological, and social needs in all decisions and actions concerning them.

However, it is important to note that the modern interpretation of "community" often differs significantly from the traditional Xhosa understanding. As discussed in *The Homeschooling Father*, the concept of community has been co-opted by some to justify the state's role in child-rearing and education, often at the expense of parental autonomy and cultural values. This modern interpretation of community, which emphasises the state's role over that of the family, can undermine the very essence of traditional child-rearing practices that prioritise the child's connection to their family, community, and cultural heritage.

1.4. The Clash with Colonial and Apartheid Systems

The arrival of European colonists in South Africa profoundly disrupted traditional child-rearing practices, imposing Western values and norms on African societies. Colonial and apartheid regimes implemented policies that systematically undermined the authority of traditional leaders and institutions, including those crucial for child welfare.

One of the most significant disruptions was the migrant labour system. This system compelled many Xhosa men from the Transkei to leave their families to work in mines and factories, often far from home. This separation destabilised traditional family structures and left women and children to cope with the absence of fathers. The support of the extended family was crucial; without it, many women would have faced the daunting challenge of raising children alone. However, the extended family could not fully compensate for the absence of fathers, who, due to dangerous working conditions, political violence, or other factors, often saw their children only sporadically, if at all. Tragically, many fathers never returned home, leaving children without parental guidance and support, especially those who did not have the benefit of father figures in the extended family.

The colonial legal system further eroded traditional child-rearing practices by imposing foreign legal doctrines that did not consider the cultural context of African families. Key among these were the **maternal preference rule** and the **tender years doctrine**, imported from English common law. These doctrines favoured mothers in custody disputes, often disregarding the traditional African understanding of child-rearing, which typically involved the broader community and extended family in caregiving roles.

1.5. The Influence of Religion and Philosophy

Religious and philosophical thought continued to influence the development of child welfare principles during the mediaeval period and beyond. The Enlightenment, with its emphasis on reason and individual rights, led to a greater recognition of children as autonomous beings with their own needs and interests.

Philosophers like John Locke and Jean-Jacques Rousseau argued for the importance of education and nurturing in child development. Locke's concept of the "tabula rasa" suggested that children are born as blank slates, and their experiences and environment shape their character and potential. Rousseau, in his book Emile, or On Education, advocated for a child-centred approach to education that respected the natural curiosity and developmental stages of children.

These philosophical ideas, along with the growing influence of humanitarian movements, led to the development of modern child welfare principles. The 20th century saw the emergence of international treaties and declarations, such as the United Nations Convention on the Rights of the Child (UNCRC), which codified the best interests of the child principle as a fundamental human right.

1.6. A Path Forward: Beyond Redress

As we trace the origins of child welfare concepts through ancient and mediaeval times, we see the gradual emergence of ideas that would later inform the best interests of the child principle. From the legal protections in Hammurabi's Code to the communal child-rearing practices in African societies, these early approaches to child welfare laid the foundation for more comprehensive child rights frameworks.

However, it's crucial to note that many of these historical practices, while progressive for their time, still fell far short of modern standards of child protection and rights. The journey from these early conceptions to the robust child rights principles we advocate for in post-apartheid South Africa is long and complex.

In the following chapters, we will explore how these ancient and mediaeval ideas evolved into modern child welfare principles, and ultimately, how the best interests of the child concept can be leveraged to address the unique challenges facing South African children today. By understanding this historical context, we can better appreciate the significance of enshrining children's rights in our constitution and the potential for these rights to drive societal transformation, moving *Beyond Redress* towards a truly equitable future.

Part II: Traditional African Child-Rearing Practices

2. From Enlightenment to Modern Era - The Evolution of Child Rights

As we move from ancient and mediaeval concepts of child welfare to more modern interpretations, we witness a remarkable transformation in how society views children and their rights. This chapter explores the journey from the Enlightenment period to the present day, highlighting key developments that have shaped our current understanding of the best interests of the child principle.

2.1. The Enlightenment's Child: Reshaping Perceptions

The Enlightenment era brought about significant changes in how children were perceived. John Locke's concept of the child as a "blank slate" or "tabula rasa" revolutionised thinking about child development. However misguided this approach may have been, as demonstrated by Steven Pinker in his book The Blank Slate, this notion had profound implications for education and child-rearing practices. It emphasised the importance of nurturing and positive experiences during a child's formative years.

Enlightenment thinkers laid the groundwork for recognizing children as individuals with unique needs and rights, rather than merely as small adults or property of their parents.

As these ideas spread, society began to push back against the exploitation of children. The concept of childhood as a distinct and valuable phase of life began to take hold, leading to early efforts to protect children from labour abuses and provide them with education.

2.2. Industrial Revolution and Its Aftermath

The Industrial Revolution highlighted the exploitation of children. As factories proliferated across Europe and North America, child labour became widespread. Children as young as 3 years old were employed in hazardous jobs, such as chimney sweeping. This profession, dominated by boys, exposed them to dangerous conditions that often led to severe health issues, including cancer, and sometimes resulted in workplace fatalities. Many children aged five or six endured long work hours in perilous environments, severely compromising their health and development. This grim reality catalysed reform movements and led to the introduction of the first factory acts, which began regulating child labour.

Alongside these labour reforms, a push for universal education gained momentum. Reformers argued that all children, regardless of social class, should have access to basic education. This led to the introduction of compulsory schooling laws in many countries, marking a significant step forward in recognizing the rights of children to education and protection from exploitation.

The 19th century also saw the emergence of child protection societies and early child welfare legislation. These organisations and laws aimed to safeguard children from abuse and neglect, reflecting a growing societal commitment to child welfare.

2.3. The 20th Century: Formalizing Child Rights

The horrors of World War I brought the vulnerability of children in conflict situations to the forefront of international concern. In 1924, the League of Nations, which was replaced by The United Nations after World War II adopted the Geneva Declaration of the Rights of the Child, the first international document to recognize that children had specific rights. This declaration laid out five basic principles, including the right to proper development, both materially and spiritually.

World War II further underscored the need for international cooperation in protecting children. The post-war period saw an increased emphasis on children's psychological well-being, recognizing the deep trauma many had experienced during the conflict. This shift in focus would have lasting implications for how we understand child welfare.

In 1959, the United Nations adopted the Declaration of the Rights of the Child, expanding on the principles laid out in the Geneva Declaration. This new declaration explicitly stated that the child's best interests should be a paramount consideration in all matters concerning children. It marked a significant step towards global recognition of children's rights and the best interests principle.

2.4. The UN Convention on the Rights of the Child

The crowning achievement in the evolution of child rights came in 1989 with the adoption of the UN Convention on the Rights of the Child (UNCRC). This comprehensive treaty, ratified by all UN member states except the United States, set out a wide range of rights for children. It established four core principles: non-discrimination; devotion to the best interests of the child; the right to life, survival, and development; and respect for the views of the child.

The UNCRC went beyond previous declarations by creating mechanisms for implementation and monitoring. It established the Committee on the Rights of the Child to oversee progress and hold states accountable for their commitments to children's rights.

2.5. Further Developments in Child Rights in Africa, with a Focus on South Africa

Following the adoption of the United Nations Convention on the Rights of the Child (UNCRC) in 1989, Africa made significant strides in advancing children's rights through regional instruments and national legislation. The African Charter on the Rights and Welfare of the Child (ACRWC), adopted in 1990 and entering into force in 1999, stands out as a pivotal development in this regard.

South Africa has emerged as a leader in children's rights on the African continent, distinguishing itself through robust constitutional protections and progressive legislation. The country's approach to children's rights is characterized by:

- **Constitutional Enshrinement:** South Africa's 1996 Constitution explicitly recognizes children's rights in Section 28, providing a strong legal foundation for child protection.
- **Comprehensive Legislation:** The Children's Act of 2005 and the Child Justice Act of 2008 offer detailed frameworks for child welfare and juvenile justice, respectively.
- **Judicial Interpretation:** South African courts have consistently applied the 'best interests of the child' principle, contributing to a rich body of case law that often serves as a reference for other African nations.
- **Ratification of International Instruments:** South Africa has ratified both the UNCRC and the ACRWC, demonstrating its commitment to international child rights standards.
- **Innovative Programs:** The country has implemented various child-focused initiatives, such as the Child Support Grant, which has significantly reduced child poverty.

While South Africa has made considerable progress, the situation across the rest of Africa varies:

1. **Legislative Frameworks:** Many African countries have enacted child rights legislation, but implementation often lags behind South Africa's more robust enforcement mechanisms.
2. **Resource Allocation:** South Africa generally allocates more resources to child-centric programs compared to many other African nations, which often face severe budgetary constraints.
3. **Child Labor:** While child labor remains a challenge in South Africa, particularly in agricultural settings, the country has made more progress in combating this issue compared to many other African nations where child labor in mining, agriculture,

and informal sectors remains pervasive.

4. **Education Access:** South Africa has achieved near-universal primary education enrollment, outperforming many African countries where access to education remains a significant challenge.
5. **Child Marriage:** South Africa has stricter laws and enforcement against child marriage compared to several other African countries where the practice remains prevalent.
6. **Child Soldiers:** Unlike some conflict-affected African nations, South Africa does not face the issue of child soldiers, having signed the Optional Protocol to the Convention on the Rights of the Child on the involvement of children in armed conflict.

2.6. Challenges and Critiques in the Modern Era

Despite these advances, the implementation of child rights faces significant challenges. Debates around cultural relativism versus universal rights continue, as does the struggle to balance traditional practices with international standards. Many countries face resource constraints that hinder the full realisation of child rights.

New issues have also emerged, such as children's digital rights. These challenges require innovative approaches and a renewed commitment to putting children's best interests at the forefront of policy and decision-making.

As we conclude this journey from the Enlightenment to the modern era, we see how dramatically the concept of child rights and the best interests principle have evolved. While significant progress has been made in recognizing and protecting children's rights, much work remains. The next chapter will explore how these global developments have influenced and been influenced by South African perspectives on child welfare, setting the stage for our discussion on the role of the best interests principle in addressing contemporary challenges in post-apartheid South Africa.

3. Colonial and Early South African Context: Disrupting the Child's Compass

The arrival of European colonists in South Africa marked a turning point in the nation's history, bringing with it profound changes to the social, cultural, and legal landscape. This chapter delves into the colonial impact on child welfare, examining how Western legal systems and ideologies clashed with traditional African practices, ultimately disrupting the delicate balance that had long guided child-rearing in indigenous communities. We will also explore the early South African legal landscape, highlighting the policies and practices that shaped the treatment of children before the advent of significant legal reforms.

3.1. Colonial Impact on Child Welfare

The imposition of European legal systems and cultural norms on African societies had far-reaching consequences for child welfare. Colonial powers often viewed African customs and traditions as primitive or uncivilised, seeking to replace them with Western ideals and practices. This cultural imperialism extended to child-rearing, where traditional communal approaches were often undermined or dismissed in favour of European notions of family and childhood.

One of the most significant impacts of colonialism was the introduction of Western legal concepts of guardianship and parental rights. These concepts, rooted in individualistic values, often clashed with the communal child-rearing practices prevalent in many African societies. In traditional Xhosa culture, for example, children were seen as belonging to the community as a whole, and their upbringing was a shared responsibility among family members, elders, and the broader community. The imposition of Western legal frameworks, which emphasised the nuclear family and parental authority, disrupted these traditional structures and undermined the collective responsibility for child welfare.

Furthermore, colonial laws and policies often discriminated against indigenous children, denying them access to formal education, healthcare, and other essential services. The establishment of separate schools and healthcare facilities for white and black children entrenched racial segregation and inequality, hindering the development and well-being of African children.

3.2. Early South African Practices

The early South African legal landscape, shaped by colonial and apartheid policies, further exacerbated the challenges facing children. The legal system often reflected and reinforced societal biases and discriminatory practices, particularly against black children and children from marginalised communities.

The concept of the best interests of the child, while present in some legal frameworks, was often overshadowed by discriminatory laws and practices. For example, the "Black Administration Act" of 1927 gave white Native Commissioners broad powers over African children, often leading to their removal from their families and placement in institutions or foster care with white families.

The "Children's Act" of 1960, while introducing some protections for children, also contained provisions that discriminated against black children and reinforced the authority of the state over parental rights. The Act's focus on "European" norms and values further marginalised indigenous child-rearing practices and contributed to the erosion of cultural identity.

3.3. From Colonialism to Constitution

The colonial and early South African context provides a critical backdrop for understanding the challenges and complexities of upholding the best interests of the child principle in the country today. The clash between Western legal systems and traditional African practices, coupled with the legacy of discriminatory laws and policies, has created a unique and often challenging landscape for child welfare.

As we move forward, it is essential to recognize and address the historical injustices that have shaped the lives of South African children. By acknowledging the diversity of cultural practices and values, and by working towards a more inclusive and equitable legal framework, we can create a society where the best interests of all children are truly prioritised and protected.

4. Xhosa Child-Rearing Practices: A Communal Tapestry of Nurturing and Resilience

In the heart of the Transkei region of South Africa, the Xhosa people have cultivated a rich and intricate tapestry of child-rearing practices that reflect their deep-rooted cultural values, communal spirit, and reverence for ancestral wisdom. This chapter delves into the social structures, cultural norms, and child welfare practices that have shaped the upbringing of Xhosa children for generations. By examining these traditional practices and comparing them with Western legal principles, we can gain valuable insights into the diverse approaches to child-rearing and their implications for the best interests of the child.

4.1. Overview of Xhosa Society: Ubuntu and the Collective Spirit

Xhosa society is characterised by the philosophy of *ubuntu*, a concept that emphasises interconnectedness, community, and shared responsibility. This philosophy permeates all aspects of life, including child-rearing. Children are not seen as belonging solely to their parents but are considered a precious gift from the ancestors and a collective responsibility of the entire community.

The extended family plays a central role in Xhosa child-rearing. Grandparents, aunts, uncles, and other relatives actively participate in the upbringing of children, offering guidance, support, and cultural transmission. This communal approach fosters a strong sense of belonging, identity, and social cohesion, providing children with a network of caregivers who share a vested interest in their well-being.

4.2. Child Welfare Practices: Nurturing the Next Generation

Xhosa child-rearing practices are deeply rooted in tradition and cultural values. From infancy to adulthood, children are guided through various rites of passage and rituals that mark their development and prepare them for their roles and responsibilities within the community.

- **Early Childhood:** Infants and young children are showered with affection and attention, often carried on their mothers' backs or held by other caregivers. This close physical contact fosters a strong emotional bond and a sense of security.
- **Naming Ceremonies:** The naming of a child is a significant event in Xhosa culture, often involving the participation of elders and community members. The name given to a child reflects their ancestry, family history, and hopes for their future.
- **Storytelling and Oral Tradition:** Storytelling plays a vital role in transmitting cultural knowledge, values, and history to children. Elders share folktales, proverbs, and historical narratives, instilling a sense of pride and identity in the younger generation.
- **Initiation Rites:** As children reach adolescence, they undergo initiation rites that mark their transition to adulthood. These rites, such as *ulwaluko* (circumcision for boys) and *intonjane* (initiation for girls), are deeply symbolic and serve to teach important life lessons, values, and responsibilities.
- **Communal Education:** Education in traditional Xhosa society was a continuous process of learning from elders, family members, and the community. Children learned practical skills, such as farming, animal husbandry, and crafts, and cultural traditions, social norms, and spiritual beliefs.

4.3. Comparative Analysis: Traditional vs. Western

Approaches

The Xhosa approach to child-rearing, with its emphasis on communal care, cultural transmission, and holistic development, contrasts sharply with Western legal principles like the tender years doctrine and maternal preference. These Western principles, rooted in individualistic values and gender stereotypes, often prioritise the mother's role in child-rearing and can undermine the involvement of fathers and extended family members.

The tender years doctrine, which presumes that young children are best cared for by their mothers, is at odds with the Xhosa tradition of shared parenting, where multiple caregivers contribute to a child's upbringing. Similarly, the maternal preference rule, which favours mothers in custody disputes, can marginalise the role of fathers and other family members who play a vital role in the child's life.

While Western legal principles have evolved to recognize the importance of both parents in a child's life, the legacy of the tender years doctrine and maternal preference rule continues to influence judicial decisions and societal attitudes towards parenting. This can lead to conflicts and misunderstandings in cases involving Xhosa families, where the court's understanding of the child's best interests may not align with the cultural context and values of the community.

In contrast, the Xhosa approach to child-rearing aligns more closely with the holistic and child-centric approach advocated for by the best interests of the child principle. By recognizing the importance of family, community, and cultural identity in child development, the Xhosa tradition offers valuable insights into how to create a nurturing and supportive environment that fosters the well-being and potential of every child.

5. Traditional Child-Rearing Across African Tribes: A Tapestry of Shared Values and Diverse Practices

The tapestry of African cultures is rich and diverse, woven with threads of unique traditions, beliefs, and practices. Child-rearing, a cornerstone of any society, is no exception. This chapter explores the diverse child-rearing practices across various African tribes and communities, highlighting both the common threads that bind them and the unique expressions that reflect their distinct identities. By examining these practices, we can gain a deeper understanding of the values and beliefs that shape African childhoods and their relevance to the best interests of the child principle.

5.1. A Kaleidoscope of Traditions

Across the vast continent of Africa, child-rearing practices vary significantly, reflecting the unique cultural, social, and environmental contexts of different communities. From the nomadic pastoralists of the Sahel to the agricultural communities of the Great Lakes region, each tribe has developed its own customs and traditions for raising children.

Some common themes emerge across these diverse practices. The importance of family and community is a recurring motif, with children often raised in extended family networks that provide a sense of belonging, identity, and support. Elders play a crucial role in transmitting cultural knowledge, values, and traditions to younger generations, ensuring the continuity of cultural heritage.

However, there are also significant differences in child-rearing practices across different tribes. These differences can be seen in the roles and responsibilities assigned to children, the methods of discipline and guidance, and the rituals and ceremonies that mark important milestones in a child's life.

For example, among the Maasai of East Africa, children are expected to take on responsibilities such as herding livestock and assisting with household chores from a young age. This early involvement in family and community life fosters a sense of responsibility and self-reliance.

In contrast, among the Akan people of West Africa, children are often indulged and pampered, with a strong emphasis on emotional and spiritual well-being. This nurturing approach aims to cultivate a sense of empathy, compassion, and respect for others.

5.2. Commonalities and Differences

While the specific practices may differ, there are several common threads that run through traditional African child-rearing approaches. These include:

- **Communal Care:** Children are raised in extended family networks, with multiple caregivers sharing the responsibility for their upbringing. This communal approach provides children with a sense of security, belonging, and support.
- **Cultural Transmission:** Elders play a crucial role in transmitting cultural knowledge, values, and traditions to younger generations through storytelling, rituals, and everyday interactions. This ensures the continuity of cultural heritage and strengthens the child's sense of identity.
- **Holistic Development:** Child-rearing is not just about physical care but also encompasses emotional, social, spiritual, and intellectual development. Children are encouraged to learn through experience, observation, and participation in community life.
- **Respect for Elders:** Elders are revered for their wisdom and experience, and children are taught to respect and obey them. This

respect for authority fosters discipline and social order within the community.

- **Connection to Nature:** Many African cultures have a deep connection to nature, and children are taught to respect and appreciate the natural world. This connection fosters a sense of environmental stewardship and responsibility.

These common themes reflect a holistic and child-centric approach to child-rearing that prioritises the well-being and development of the child within the context of their family and community. This approach aligns with the best interests of the child principle, which emphasises the importance of considering the child's physical, emotional, psychological, and social needs in all decisions and actions concerning them.

However, there are also notable differences in child-rearing practices across different African tribes. These differences can be attributed to various factors, including geographical location, economic activities, social structures, and religious beliefs.

For example, nomadic pastoralist communities, such as the Maasai and the Fulani, tend to have more gender-segregated roles for children, with boys focusing on herding and girls on domestic chores. In contrast, agricultural communities, such as the Akan and the Yoruba, may have more flexible gender roles, with both boys and girls participating in farming and other activities.

The methods of discipline and guidance also vary across cultures. Some communities may use corporal punishment, while others rely on verbal reprimands, storytelling, or community sanctions to correct children's behaviour.

5.3. Comparing with Xhosa Practices

The Xhosa child-rearing practices discussed in the previous chapter share many similarities with those of other African tribes. The emphasis on communal care, cultural transmission, and holistic development is a common thread that runs through many African cultures.

However, there are also some unique aspects of Xhosa child-rearing that distinguish it from other traditions. For example, the Xhosa initiation rites, *ulwaluko* and *intonjane*, are particularly elaborate and play a central role in the transition from childhood to adulthood. These rites serve not only as a marker of maturity but also as a means of transmitting cultural knowledge, values, and social responsibilities.

The Xhosa tradition of *ubuntu*, with its emphasis on interconnectedness and shared responsibility, also has a profound impact on child-rearing practices. Children are raised to value community and to understand their role in contributing to the well-being of others. This communal ethos fosters a sense of empathy, compassion, and social responsibility that is essential for building a harmonious and equitable society.

By comparing Xhosa child-rearing practices with those of other African tribes, we can gain a deeper appreciation for the diversity and richness of African cultures. We can also identify common themes and values that can inform our understanding of the best interests of the child principle and its application in the South African context.

Part III: The Best Interests of the Child in South African Law

6. The Legal Transformation: Embracing the Best Interests of the Child in South African Law

The dawn of democracy in South Africa in 1994 ushered in a transformative era for the nation's legal landscape, particularly in the realm of child welfare and protection. The newly adopted Constitution, a beacon of hope and progress, enshrined the principle of the best interests of the child as a fundamental cornerstone of the legal framework. This chapter explores the integration of this principle into South African law, examining its constitutional enshrinement and its profound implications for the rights and well-being of children.

6.1. Introduction to the Best Interests Principle in South Africa

The best interests of the child principle, a concept that had been evolving for centuries in various legal and cultural contexts, found a firm footing in South African law with the enactment of the 1994 Constitution. This principle, which prioritises the child's well-being in all matters concerning them, marked a significant departure from the previous legal framework that often favoured maternal rights and perpetuated gender stereotypes.

The inclusion of the best interests principle in the Constitution was a testament to the nation's commitment to protecting the rights of its most vulnerable citizens. It recognized that children are not merely passive recipients of care but are rights-holders with inherent dignity and agency. This principle, enshrined in Section 28 of the Bill of Rights, mandates that in all matters concerning children, their best interests shall be of paramount importance.

6.2. Constitutional Enshrinement: Section 28 and Its

Significance

Section 28 of the Bill of Rights is a comprehensive and powerful provision that outlines a wide range of rights and protections for children. It encompasses their right to a name and nationality, family care or appropriate alternative care, basic nutrition, shelter, healthcare, and social services. It also protects children from maltreatment, neglect, abuse, and exploitation.

However, the most significant aspect of Section 28 is its unequivocal declaration that "a child's best interests are of paramount importance in every matter concerning the child." This principle serves as the guiding light for all decisions and actions that affect children, whether in the context of family law, child protection, education, or healthcare.

The constitutional enshrinement of the best interests principle has had a profound impact on the South African legal landscape. It has led to the development of new laws and policies that prioritise the well-being of children.

The principle has also influenced judicial decision-making, with courts increasingly applying a child-centric approach in cases involving custody, access, and other child-related matters. This has led to a greater recognition of the importance of both parents in a child's life, regardless of their gender or marital status, and a move away from the traditional maternal preference rule that favoured mothers in custody disputes.

The best interests of the child principle has also played a crucial role in challenging discriminatory practices and policies that harm children's well-being. For example, in the case of *Goliath's Stand*, the principle is being used to argue against the discriminatory practices of the Children's Court, which often marginalised fathers and denied them equal parental rights.

6.3. The Best Interests of the Child and Equality Before the Law

The principle of the best interests of the child is not only a cornerstone of child protection but also aligns seamlessly with the fundamental principle of equality before the law. This alignment is crucial in ensuring that children's rights are upheld without discrimination based on gender or other factors.

Equality before the law, as enshrined in Section 9(1) of the Constitution, guarantees that all individuals are equal before the law and have the right to equal protection and benefit of the law. This principle prohibits unfair discrimination on various grounds, including race, gender, sex, pregnancy, marital status, ethnic or social origin, colour, sexual orientation, age, disability, religion, conscience, belief, culture, language, and birth.

In the context of child custody and care, the best interests of the child principle, in conjunction with the equality clause, mandates that courts cannot discriminate between parents based on their gender. This means that both mothers and fathers have equal rights and responsibilities towards their children, and decisions regarding custody, access, and care must be made solely based on what is in the best interests of the child, without any gender bias.

Furthermore, the best interests of the child principle requires a focus on the child's individual circumstances, taking into account their unique needs, preferences, and relationships with both parents. This individualised approach is consistent with the principle of equality before the law, as it ensures that each child is treated as a unique individual, rather than being subjected to generalisations or stereotypes based on their parents' gender.

This alignment between the best interests of the child principle and equality before the law has significant implications for challenging discriminatory practices and policies. For instance, broad-based policies like affirmative action, which prioritise certain groups based on race or gender, can be argued to be in conflict with both the best interests of the child and the principle of equality before the law. Such policies may inadvertently discriminate against children who do not fall within the designated groups, limiting their opportunities and potential based on factors beyond their control.

By upholding the best interests of the child principle and the principle of equality before the law, South Africa can create a legal and social environment that is truly fair and equitable for all children. This requires a commitment to dismantling discriminatory practices, promoting equal parenting rights, and ensuring that every child has the opportunity to thrive, regardless of their background or circumstances.

7. Pre-Constitutional Legal Principles: A Legacy of Gender Bias

Before the transformative 1994 Constitution, South African family law was heavily influenced by Western legal principles that often perpetuated gender stereotypes and inequalities. This chapter delves into two such principles—the tender years doctrine and the maternal preference principle—examining their history, application, and ultimate incompatibility with both traditional African practices and the constitutional guarantee of equality before the law.

7.1. The Tender Years Doctrine: A Presumption of Maternal Superiority

The tender years doctrine, a legal principle rooted in English common law, operated under the presumption that young children, particularly those of "tender years" (typically under the age of seven), were best cared for by their mothers. This doctrine stemmed from societal norms that viewed women as the primary caregivers and men as breadwinners. While seemingly benign, this doctrine had far-reaching consequences for child custody decisions, often resulting in fathers being marginalised and denied equal parental rights.

In South Africa, the tender years doctrine was adopted and applied in various forms throughout the 20th century. Courts often relied on this principle to award custody to mothers, even in cases where fathers were equally capable and willing to care for their children. This bias towards mothers not only perpetuated gender stereotypes but also disregarded the diverse family structures and child-rearing practices prevalent in many African cultures.

7.2. The Maternal Preference Principle: Reinforcing Gender Stereotypes

The maternal preference principle, closely related to the tender years doctrine, further reinforced the notion that mothers were the natural and preferred caregivers for young children. This principle was often invoked in custody disputes, where courts would prioritise the mother's claim to custody, even in the absence of evidence of her superior parenting abilities.

The maternal preference principle had a profound impact on the lives of fathers and children. Fathers were often relegated to the role of secondary caregivers, with limited access to their children and little say in their upbringing. This not only denied fathers their rightful role in their children's lives but also deprived children of the benefits of having a close and meaningful relationship with both parents.

7.3. Compatibility and Conflict: Traditional Practices vs. Western Principles

The tender years doctrine and maternal preference principle were not only discriminatory against fathers but also clashed with traditional African child-rearing practices. In many African cultures, child-rearing is a communal responsibility, with extended family members, including grandparents, aunts, uncles, and siblings, playing an active role in the upbringing of children.

The Xhosa tradition, for example, emphasises the importance of *ubuntu*, a philosophy of interconnectedness and shared responsibility. Children are seen as belonging to the community as a whole, and their upbringing is a collective effort. The imposition of Western legal principles that prioritised the mother's role undermined this communal approach and disrupted the traditional support systems that had long nurtured and protected children.

7.4. Incompatibility with Equality Before the Law

The tender years doctrine and maternal preference principle also contradicted the fundamental principle of equality before the law. By favouring mothers over fathers in custody disputes, these principles perpetuated gender stereotypes and denied fathers equal protection and benefit of the law.

The 1994 Constitution, with its emphasis on equality and non-discrimination, paved the way for dismantling these discriminatory principles. The constitutional enshrinement of the best interests of the child principle, which requires a holistic and individualised assessment of each child's needs and circumstances, further reinforced the need to move away from gender-based presumptions in child custody decisions.

Landmark court cases, such as *Fraser v Children's Court, Pretoria North* (1997) and *M v M* (2008), challenged and ultimately overturned the tender years doctrine and maternal preference principle. These rulings affirmed the importance of considering the child's best interests above all else, regardless of the parent's gender.

The rejection of these discriminatory principles marked a significant step towards achieving gender equality in family law and child welfare. It recognized that both mothers and fathers have an equal right and responsibility to care for their children, and that decisions regarding custody and access should be based on the child's individual needs and the capacity of each parent to provide for those needs.

8. Case Law and Judicial Interpretation

The best interests of the child principle, enshrined in Section 28 of the South African Constitution, has been a driving force in numerous landmark court cases that have shaped the landscape of child welfare and protection in the country. These cases have not only clarified the meaning and scope of the principle but also demonstrated its power to challenge discriminatory practices and promote the well-being of children.

- ***S v M* (2007):** This case involved a dispute between a lesbian couple and the biological father of a child born through artificial insemination. The Constitutional Court held that the best interests of the child were paramount and that both the biological and social parents had a role to play in the child's life. This decision affirmed the importance of considering the child's relationship with all relevant caregivers, regardless of their sexual orientation or marital status.
- ***Centre for Child Law v Minister of Social Development* (2009):** This case challenged the constitutionality of certain provisions of the Children's Act that discriminated against children born out of wedlock. The Constitutional Court ruled that these provisions were unconstitutional as they violated children's rights to equality and dignity. This decision affirmed the principle that all children, regardless of their parents' marital status, are entitled to equal protection and benefit of the law.
- ***FS v JJ and Others* (2011):** This case involved a dispute between a divorced couple over the relocation of their child. The Supreme Court of Appeal held that the best interests of the child should be the primary consideration in relocation cases, and that courts should consider a wide range of factors, including the child's views, the relationship between the child and each parent, and the impact of the relocation on the child's well-being.

• ***JT v Road Accident Fund* (2015):** This case involved a claim for damages on behalf of a child who had been injured in a car accident. The Constitutional Court held that the best interests of the child should be the primary consideration in determining the amount of damages awarded, and that courts should consider the child's future needs, including medical expenses, rehabilitation, and loss of earning capacity.

These landmark cases demonstrate the transformative power of the best interests of the child principle in South African law. They have challenged discriminatory practices, expanded the scope of children's rights, and ensured that the child's well-being is prioritised in all legal decisions that affect them.

8.1. Judicial Trends: A Child-Centric Approach

The best interests of the child principle has not only influenced landmark court decisions but has also shaped broader judicial trends in South Africa. Courts are increasingly adopting a child-centric approach, recognizing children as active participants in their own lives and giving due consideration to their views and preferences.

This shift is evident in various areas of law, including:

• **Custody and Access Disputes:** Courts are moving away from the traditional maternal preference rule and focusing on the individual needs and circumstances of each child. They are increasingly considering shared parenting arrangements and recognizing the importance of both parents in a child's life.

• **Child Protection Cases:** Courts are prioritising the safety and well-being of children in cases of abuse, neglect, and exploitation. They are taking a more proactive approach to child protection, intervening early to prevent harm and ensuring that children receive the necessary support and services.

• **Adoption and Foster Care:** Courts are placing greater emphasis on finding permanent, stable, and loving homes for children in need of care. They are also recognizing the importance of maintaining cultural and familial connections for children in alternative care.

These judicial trends reflect a growing recognition of the importance of the best interests of the child principle in all aspects of child welfare and protection. By adopting a child-centric approach, courts are not only upholding the rights of children but also contributing to the creation of a more just and equitable society for all.

Part IV: The Contemporary Application and Challenges

9. Legislative Reforms and State Spending

The best interests of the child principle has had a profound impact on South African legislation and state spending since its enshrinement in the Constitution. This chapter examines how this principle has shaped legislative reforms and influenced the allocation of government resources towards children's welfare.

9.1. Impact on Legislation

The best interests principle has been a driving force behind several significant legislative reforms in South Africa:

- Children's Act 38 of 2005: This comprehensive legislation overhauled the legal framework for child protection in South Africa. It emphasises the best interests of the child in all matters concerning children, including adoption, foster care, and child custody.
- Child Justice Act 75 of 2008: This act reformed the criminal justice system for children in conflict with the law, prioritising rehabilitation and reintegration over punitive measures.
- South African Schools Act 84 of 1996 (as amended): Reforms to this act have focused on ensuring equal access to education and protecting children's rights within the school system.
- Social Assistance Act 13 of 2004: This act provides for social grants, including the Child Support Grant, which has been crucial in supporting children from low-income families.

These legislative reforms demonstrate a clear shift towards a child-centric approach in South African law, with the best interests principle serving as a guiding framework.

9.2. State Spending and Resource Allocation

The South African government has established several entities dedicated to protecting children's interests and has allocated significant resources to support children's welfare:

- Department of Social Development: Annual budget for 2021/2022 was approximately R205 billion, with a significant portion dedicated to child welfare services and grants.
- Department of Basic Education: Annual budget for 2021/2022 was about R279 billion, focused on providing education and related services to children.
- Office of the Rights of the Child (in the Presidency): While specific budget figures are not readily available, this office plays a crucial role in coordinating child rights policies across government departments.
- South African Human Rights Commission: While not exclusively focused on children, it has a dedicated children's rights unit. Its total annual budget for 2021/2022 was approximately R189 million.
- National Child Protection Committee: An inter-sectoral body coordinating child protection efforts, though specific budget allocations are not publicly detailed.

9.3. Spending on Parents

While precise figures are difficult to isolate, a stark disparity exists in government spending aimed at supporting mothers versus fathers as parents. This imbalance not only perpetuates gender stereotypes but also raises concerns about the equitable application of the best interests of the child principle.

- **Maternity Benefits:** The Unemployment Insurance Fund (UIF) provides maternity benefits for up to 17.32 weeks, with a substantial R1.6 billion disbursed in the 2020/2021 financial year.
- **Child Support Grant:** Although accessible to both parents, this grant, amounting to R480 per month per child as of 2023, is

predominantly claimed by mothers. In 2021/2022, a significant R71.3 billion was allocated to these grants.

- **Paternity Leave:** While fathers are entitled to 10 days of paternity leave since 2019, paid through the UIF, the allocated budget and actual spending on this benefit are notably less than maternity benefits.
- **Father-Specific Programs:** A glaring absence of government programs and dedicated spending specifically designed to support fathers in their parenting roles further underscores the systemic neglect of fathers' contributions to child-rearing.

This skewed allocation of resources not only reflects a disregard for fathers' roles in their children's lives but also raises questions about the state's commitment to upholding the best interests of the child. A child thrives best when nurtured and supported by both parents. By neglecting to invest in fathers, the government inadvertently undermines the well-being of children who are deprived of the full benefits of paternal involvement.

Furthermore, this disparity in spending can be seen as a form of indirect discrimination against children in families where fathers are the primary caregivers. When fathers lack access to the same resources and support as mothers, their ability to provide for their children's needs is compromised, ultimately affecting the children's overall well-being.

The lack of investment in fathers also perpetuates harmful gender stereotypes that can have long-term consequences for children's development. When boys grow up seeing their fathers marginalised and excluded from the parenting narrative, it can negatively impact their own understanding of fatherhood and masculinity.

10. Failures in Prioritising the Best Interests of the Child

The best interests of the child principle, enshrined in Section 28 of the South African Constitution, is a powerful mandate that should guide all decisions and actions affecting children. However, the prioritisation of redress policies and state-sanctioned discrimination has often led to unintended consequences that undermine this fundamental principle. This chapter examines how the pursuit of redress, while aiming to address historical injustices, has sometimes conflicted with the best interests of the child, resulting in real-world impacts on children's lives and well-being. It also explores the role of the High Court as the upper guardian of all children and its failure to adequately address discriminatory practices and laws that are not in the best interests of the child.

10.1. Redress Provision vs. Best Interests: A Conflict of Priorities

The redress provision in Section 9(2) of the Constitution allows for measures to promote equality and address past discrimination. However, the implementation of these measures, often in the form of affirmative action and Black Economic Empowerment (BEE) policies, has raised concerns about their compatibility with the best interests of the child principle.

While redress policies aim to create a more equitable society, they often rely on broad-based categorizations based on race or gender. This approach can overlook the individual needs and circumstances of children, leading to unintended consequences that may harm their well-being. For example, affirmative action policies in education and employment may limit opportunities for children from non-designated groups, regardless of their individual merit or potential.

Furthermore, the focus on redress can sometimes overshadow the importance of other factors that contribute to a child's well-being, such as stable family structures, access to quality education and healthcare, and a nurturing environment. By prioritising group-based redress over the individual needs of children, these policies may inadvertently perpetuate inequality and hinder the full realisation of the best interests of the child principle.

10.2. Real-World Impacts: The Born-Free Generation's Burden

The negative consequences of prioritising redress over the best interests of the child are evident in the experiences of the "born-free" generation, those born after the end of apartheid. Despite the promise of a more equitable society, this generation faces significant challenges, including high unemployment rates, rampant crime, and a lack of opportunities.

As highlighted in "The Unfairness of Fair Discrimination in South Africa," the burden of redress policies often falls disproportionately on the shoulders of the "born-frees." They are the ones who bear the brunt of affirmative action policies that limit their employment prospects and economic opportunities. They are also the ones who suffer from the unintended consequences of BEE policies, such as corruption and cronyism, which divert resources away from essential services like education and healthcare.

The high unemployment rate among the "born-frees" is a particularly alarming indicator of the failure of redress policies to create a truly equitable society. While these policies may have benefited a small elite within the designated groups, they have not translated into widespread economic empowerment for the majority of black South Africans.

10.3. The High Court's Role: A Failure of Guardianship?

The High Court, as the upper guardian of all children in South Africa, has a constitutional duty to protect their rights and ensure their well-being. However, the court's track record in addressing discriminatory practices and laws that are not in the best interests of the child has been mixed.

In some cases, the High Court has upheld the constitutionality of redress policies, even when they have been challenged on the grounds of discrimination. For example, in the case of *Minister of Finance v Van Heerden* (2004), the court upheld an affirmative action policy that provided more favourable pension benefits to black employees, despite arguments that it discriminated against white employees.

However, in other cases, the court has recognized the potential conflict between redress policies and the best interests of the child. In *AB and Another v Minister of Social Development* (2016), the court acknowledged the discriminatory impact of a law requiring a genetic link in surrogacy agreements, but ultimately upheld the law due to concerns about the child's right to know their genetic origins.

The High Court's reluctance to strike down discriminatory laws, even when they conflict with the best interests of the child, raises questions about its commitment to upholding this fundamental principle. The court's decisions often reflect a balancing act between competing rights and interests, but the prioritisation of redress over the well-being of children can have long-term consequences for their development and future prospects.

The High Court's failure to consistently and effectively challenge discriminatory practices and laws that harm children's interests is a significant concern. As the upper guardian of all children, the court has a responsibility to ensure that their rights are protected and that their well-being is prioritised in all legal and policy decisions. This requires a more proactive and assertive approach to judicial review, one that recognizes the potential harm caused by discriminatory policies and prioritises the best interests of the child above all else.

11. The Reality of the Born Frees

The "Born Free" generation, those born after the end of apartheid in 1994, were meant to inherit a South Africa free from the shackles of racial discrimination and inequality. This chapter examines the reality faced by this generation, analysing South Africa's progress and failures over the past three decades and how redress policies have shaped their opportunities and challenges.

11.1. Review of Key Performance Areas (1994-2024)

11.1.1. Education

- Progress
  - Increased access to basic education, with near-universal enrollment in primary schools
  - Introduction of no-fee schools and school nutrition programs
- Failures
  - Persistent inequality in education quality between former Model C schools and township/rural schools
  - Poor performance in international assessments (e.g., PIRLS, TIMSS)
  - High dropout rates, especially at the secondary level
- Statistics

○ Matric pass rate increased from 58% in 1994 to 82.7% in 2023.

○ However, only 38.4% of matric candidates achieved bachelor's passes in 2023

11.1.2. Employment

- Progress

○ Implementation of affirmative action and Black Economic Empowerment (BEE) policies

○ Expansion of public sector employment

- Failures

○ Persistently high unemployment rates, especially among youth
○ Skills mismatch between education outputs and job market needs
○ Slow economic growth limiting job creation

- Statistics

○ Youth unemployment rate (15-24 years) stood at 61.4% in Q4 2023
○ Overall unemployment rate increased from 20% in 1994 to 32.1% in Q4 2023

11.1.3. Social Stability

- Progress

○ Expansion of social grant system, reducing extreme poverty

  - ○ Improved access to basic services (electricity, water, sanitation).

- Failures

  - ○ High crime rates and perceived lack of personal safety

  - ○ Persistent inequality, with South Africa remaining one of the most unequal countries globally

  - ○ Social unrest and service delivery protests.

- Statistics

  - ○ Gini coefficient (measure of inequality) remained high at 0.63 in 2023

  - ○ 17.9 million South Africans received social grants in 2023, up from 4 million in 1994

11.2. Impact of Redress Policies on the Born Free Generation

Redress policies, while aimed at addressing historical injustices, have had mixed outcomes for the born free generation. Affirmative action, Black Economic Empowerment (BEE), and preferential procurement were designed to rectify racial inequalities across various sectors. These policies have led to increased representation of historically disadvantaged groups in certain sectors and corporate leadership roles, and improved access to higher education through bursaries and scholarships targeted at previously disadvantaged individuals. They have also supported the creation of black-owned businesses, providing opportunities for entrepreneurship among the born frees.

However, these policies have often benefited a small, connected elite rather than broadly improving opportunities for the majority of born frees. The intended economic redistribution has sometimes led to market distortions, creating dependencies and inefficiencies that undermine broader economic development. Moreover, affirmative action and preferential policies have generated perceptions of reverse discrimination, fostering tensions between different racial groups. Despite the focus on redress, significant poverty and unemployment persist, particularly among those not directly benefiting from these policies.

A pertinent example is affirmative action in higher education. Policies designed to increase the enrollment of historically disadvantaged students in universities have improved access for some but have also sparked debates about merit and equality. Many born frees feel these policies have not adequately addressed systemic issues in the education system, leading to a mismatch between qualifications and employment opportunities.

11.3. The Unintended Legacy: A Call for Objective Reassessment

The reality facing South Africa's Born Free generation starkly contrasts with the aspirations that heralded the end of apartheid. Far from inheriting a society of equal opportunity, many of these young South Africans find themselves trapped in a cycle of poverty and disadvantage, perpetuated by the very policies intended to address historical injustices.

The ripple effects of race and gender-based legislation have extended beyond the Born Frees themselves, impacting their children and, in some cases, even their grandchildren. This intergenerational burden is compounded by the economic strain placed on young South Africans who must support not only their own families but also their parents, many of whom were marginalised by discriminatory policies. The cruel irony is that these youth often struggle to meet their own basic needs, let alone those of their dependents.

Milton Friedman's wisdom resonates profoundly in this context: "One of the great mistakes is to judge policies and programs by their intentions rather than their results." After three decades of redress and affirmative action policies, it is imperative that we heed Friedman's advice. The time has come for an objective, clear-eyed assessment of these policies based on their outcomes, not their intended goals.

The data and experiences of the past 30 years provide ample evidence for such an evaluation. The persistent high unemployment rates, the widening wealth gap, and the ongoing struggles of the Born Free generation and their children all point to a troubling conclusion: in our quest to redress the injustices of the past, we have inadvertently compromised both the present and the future.

This is not to suggest that the goals of redress and equality are misguided. Rather, it is a recognition that the methods employed to achieve these goals have, in many cases, fallen short or produced unintended negative consequences. The continued use of racial classifications in policy-making, for instance, has perpetuated divisions and created new forms of exclusion, running counter to the vision of a non-racial society.

As we look to the future, it is crucial that we move beyond good intentions and focus on effective solutions. This may require a fundamental rethinking of our approach to addressing historical injustices. We must seek policies that promote genuine equality of opportunity without resorting to discriminatory practices that merely shift the burden of inequality from one group to another.

The Born Free generation, and indeed all South Africans, deserve a society that truly lives up to the promises of the post-apartheid era. This will require courage, creativity, and a willingness to challenge entrenched ideas. It will mean prioritising economic growth, education reform, and job creation over rigid quota systems. Most importantly, it will require a commitment to judging our progress not by the loftiness of our goals, but by the tangible improvements in the lives of all South Africans.

The path forward is challenging, but necessary. By learning from the unintended consequences of past policies and embracing a more nuanced, results-oriented approach, South Africa can begin to build a future that honours the sacrifices of the past while creating genuine opportunities for all its citizens, regardless of race or gender. The time for objective reassessment is now – the future of the Born Frees, their children, and the nation as a whole depends on it.

Part V: A Path Forward

12. Reforming Policy and Legal Frameworks

To truly champion the best interests of the child in post-apartheid South Africa, a comprehensive overhaul of existing policies and legal frameworks is imperative. The current landscape, marred by the unintended consequences of redress policies, necessitates a paradigm shift towards a more equitable and child-centric approach. This section outlines concrete recommendations for reform, emphasising the need to move beyond race and gender-based quotas and embrace a merit-based system that prioritises individual potential and the well-being of all children.

12.1. Merit-Based Approaches: A Path to True Equality

The pursuit of a truly equitable society requires a shift away from race and gender-based policies towards a merit-based approach that recognizes and rewards individual potential and achievement. By focusing on individual capabilities and contributions, rather than immutable characteristics, we can create a more just and inclusive society where everyone has the opportunity to succeed based on their merit.

- **Merit-Based Education:** Implement educational policies that prioritise merit and academic achievement, while also providing targeted support for disadvantaged students to ensure equal opportunities for all. This includes investing in quality education for all, regardless of socioeconomic background, and promoting a curriculum that equips students with the skills needed for the modern workforce.
- **Merit-Based Employment:** Encourage employers to adopt merit-based hiring and promotion practices that focus on qualifications, skills, and experience, rather than race or gender. This would create a more competitive and dynamic workforce, where individuals are

rewarded for their abilities and contributions, not their demographic characteristics.

- **Merit-Based Procurement:** Reform public procurement policies to prioritise merit and value for money, rather than relying on preferential treatment based on race or gender. This would ensure that government contracts are awarded to the most qualified and capable bidders, promoting efficiency, transparency, and accountability in the use of public funds.

12.2. Recommendations for Reform

To truly champion the best interests of the child in democratic South Africa, a comprehensive overhaul of existing policies and legal frameworks is imperative. The current landscape, marred by the unintended consequences of redress policies, necessitates a paradigm shift towards a more equitable and child-centric approach. This section outlines concrete recommendations for reform, emphasising the need to move beyond race and gender-based quotas and embrace a merit-based system that prioritises individual potential and the well-being of all children.

- **Comprehensive Policy Review:** To align national policies with the best interests of the child principle, it is crucial to undertake a thorough review of all existing policies and legislation. This can be achieved by establishing an independent commission tasked with scrutinising current frameworks through this critical lens. Such a commission would ensure that all policy decisions, past and present, prioritise the welfare of children. Furthermore, it should be mandated that all new policies undergo a "Child Impact Assessment" before they are implemented. This assessment would evaluate the potential effects of proposed policies on children, ensuring that their interests are safeguarded from the outset.
- **Education Reform:** In the realm of education, there is an urgent need to shift focus from race-based admission policies to systems that

support students based on their needs. This approach would involve eliminating all race- and gender-based discrimination as a criterion for eligibility, ensuring that education programs are accessible to all children, regardless of their background. Investment in teacher training and retention should be based on merit and performance, ensuring that educators are well-equipped and motivated to provide the best possible education. By concentrating resources on these areas, the education system can better serve all children and prepare them for a successful future.

- **Employment and Economic Policies:** Employment and economic policies require a significant overhaul to address the limitations of current frameworks such as Broad-Based Black Economic Empowerment (BEE). Rather than broad-based racial quotas, there should be targeted interventions focused on skills development and supporting entrepreneurship. These measures would provide meaningful assistance to those most in need, fostering a more inclusive and dynamic economy. Additionally, youth employment initiatives should be designed to address individual needs rather than relying on demographic criteria. This shift would help bridge the gap between the current workforce and the job market's demands, providing young people with the tools they need to succeed.

- **Social Welfare:** Reforming the child grant system is essential to ensure that it effectively reaches all children in need, irrespective of their parents' race or gender. This reform would involve reassessing eligibility criteria and distribution mechanisms to eliminate biases and ensure equitable access. Comprehensive support programs for young parents should also be developed, focusing on their ability to care for their children rather than their demographic characteristics. Such programs would provide practical assistance and resources to help young parents succeed, contributing to better outcomes for their children.

- **Legal Framework:** The legal framework governing children's welfare must be adjusted to prioritise the best interests of the child explicitly over redress considerations in all related matters. This adjustment would require amending the Children's Act to reflect this priority clearly. In addition, family law reforms are necessary to ensure equal treatment of both parents in legal matters concerning their children. These reforms should focus on each parent's ability to provide care, rather than adhering to outdated gender stereotypes. By doing so, the legal system can promote a more balanced and fair approach to child welfare and parental responsibilities.

Implementing these recommendations will not only address the shortcomings of current policies but will also create a more equitable environment that prioritises the well-being and development of all children in South Africa.

12.3. The Best Interests of the Child: A Paramount Consideration in All Policy Decisions

The principle of the best interests of the child, as enshrined in Section 28 of the Constitution, should not be confined to family law and child protection matters. It should be the guiding principle in all policy decisions, as every decision made by the government ultimately affects children, whether directly or indirectly.

Policies that discriminate based on race or gender, such as affirmative action and BEE, can have unintended negative consequences for children. For example, when a parent is denied a job or business opportunity due to their race, it directly impacts their ability to provide for their children, thus hindering the child's development and future prospects.

By prioritising the best interests of the child in all policy decisions, we can ensure that every child has the opportunity to thrive, regardless of their background. This means creating a level playing field where all children have equal access to education, healthcare, and economic opportunities. It also means dismantling discriminatory practices that perpetuate inequality and hamper social mobility.

The best interests of the child principle is not only a moral imperative but also a constitutional obligation. By upholding this principle, we can create a more just and equitable society for all South Africans, one where every child has the opportunity to reach their full potential.

13. Empowering Courts and Legislators

The judiciary and legislature play crucial roles in safeguarding the best interests of the child. This chapter explores how these institutions can be empowered and reformed to ensure that the principle of the best interests of the child is consistently applied and prioritised over discriminatory policies.

13.1. Upholding the Best Interests of the Child as Upper Guardian

The High Court of South Africa, as the upper guardian of all children, bears a profound responsibility to ensure the well-being and protection of the nation's youth. This role extends beyond merely adjudicating individual cases; it encompasses a duty to actively safeguard the best interests of the child in all legal and policy matters. To fulfil this mandate, the High Court must adopt a proactive and vigilant approach, scrutinising legislation, policies, and practices that may directly or indirectly impact children's lives.

One of the key ways the High Court can exercise its guardianship is through judicial review. This involves assessing the constitutionality of laws and policies, ensuring they align with the principles enshrined in the Bill of Rights, particularly Section 28, which prioritises the best interests of the child. By striking down or amending discriminatory laws, such as those that perpetuate gender bias in child custody cases, the High Court can create a legal framework that truly reflects the values of equality and justice for all children.

Furthermore, the High Court can play an active role in shaping jurisprudence by interpreting and applying the best interests of the child principle in a manner that is consistent with the evolving needs and realities of South African society. This includes recognizing the diversity of family structures, promoting equal parental responsibility, and challenging discriminatory practices that undermine the well-being of children.

The High Court can also leverage its position as the upper guardian to issue guidelines and directives to lower courts, government agencies, and other stakeholders involved in child welfare. These guidelines can help ensure that the best interests of the child are consistently prioritised in all decisions and actions affecting children, from custody disputes to the allocation of resources for education and healthcare.

13.2. Role of the Judiciary

- **Holding the High Court Accountable as Upper Guardian:**

    - Conduct a comprehensive review of the High Court's performance in upholding its role as the upper guardian of all children.

    - Ensure the High Court actively identifies legislation and actions by the government, private entities, and individuals that are not in the best interests of the child.

    - Mandate regular reports from government departments on the implementation of child-centric policies.

    - Require the High Court to report on programs implemented to fulfil its role as an upper guardian and provide regular progress reports.

- **Judicial Review of Policies:**

    - Expand the scope of judicial review to include a "best interests of the child" test for all policies, even those not directly aimed at children.

○ Develop clear judicial guidelines for applying the best interests principle in cases involving conflicting rights or policies.

- **Training and Capacity Building:**

○ Implement mandatory training for judges on child rights, child psychology, and the long-term impacts of policies on child welfare.

○ Establish a panel of expert advisors (child psychologists, educationists, social workers) to assist courts in complex cases involving children.

- **Precedent Setting:**

○ Encourage courts to set strong precedents that prioritise children's interests over discriminatory policies or practices.

○ Develop a body of case law that interprets the best interests principle broadly, considering long-term and indirect impacts on children.

- **Enforcement Powers:**

○ Grant courts enhanced powers to monitor and enforce compliance with judgments related to children's welfare.

○ Establish mechanisms for courts to impose sanctions on government departments that fail to implement child-centric policies effectively.

- **Public Interest Litigation:**

○ Encourage and facilitate public interest litigation on behalf of children's rights.

○ Establish a dedicated fund to support legal challenges that seek to uphold the best interests of children.

- **Intersectional Approach:**

○ Mandate that courts consider the intersectional impacts of policies on children, recognizing that factors like race, gender, and socioeconomic status often interact in complex ways.

13.3. Empowering Courts to Prioritise Best Interests over Discriminatory Policies

- **Constitutional Interpretation:**

○ Develop a jurisprudence that interprets Section 28 (best interests of the child) as having primacy over other constitutional provisions when they conflict.

○ Encourage courts to adopt a "child-first" approach in constitutional interpretation.

- **Burden of Proof:**

○ Shift the burden of proof to the state or parties defending potentially discriminatory policies to demonstrate that these policies do not harm children's interests.

- **Remedial Powers:**

○ Expand courts' remedial powers to include the ability to strike down or modify policies that discriminate against children, even if indirectly.

○ Empower courts to order specific remedies, such as policy reformulation or budget reallocation, to better serve children's interests.

- **Standing and Access:**

○ Broaden rules of standing to allow child advocates, NGOs, and concerned citizens to bring cases on behalf of children more easily.

○ Implement child-friendly court procedures to ensure children's voices are heard in matters affecting them.

- **Judicial Activism:**

○ Encourage a form of judicial activism that proactively seeks to protect and promote children's rights.

○ Empower judges to call for evidence or expert opinions on the potential impacts of policies on children, even when not explicitly presented by the parties.

13.4. Legislative Changes

- **Best Interests of the Child Act:**

○ Propose a comprehensive act that codifies the best interests principle and mandates its application across all areas of law and policy.

○ Include provisions that require all legislation to undergo a "child impact assessment" before enactment.

- **Amendment to the Equality Act:**

○ Modify the Promotion of Equality and Prevention of Unfair Discrimination Act to explicitly recognize the primacy of children's interests in cases of apparent conflict with other equality provisions.

- **Children's Rights Ombudsman:**

○ Establish an independent Children's Rights Ombudsman with the power to investigate, report on, and challenge policies that negatively impact children.

- **Policy Impact Assessment Act:**

○ Enact legislation requiring all government departments to conduct and publish child impact assessments for all major policy decisions.

- **Equality Before the Law Enhancement Act:**

○ Propose legislation that reinforces the principle of equality before the law, with specific provisions to protect children from both direct and indirect discrimination.

- **Child-Centric Budgeting Act:**

○ Enact a law requiring a certain percentage of the national budget to be allocated specifically to programs that directly benefit children.

○ Mandate transparency and accountability in using these funds.

- **Education Equality Act:**

○ Propose legislation that focuses on equalising educational opportunities based on individual need rather than demographic factors.

- **Family Law Reform:**

○ Amend family law statutes to prioritise the best interests of the child in all custody, maintenance, and family-related decisions.

○ Remove gender biases in family law, focusing instead on each parent's ability to meet the child's needs.

13.5. Conclusion

Empowering courts and legislators to prioritise the best interests of the child is crucial for creating a more equitable and child-centric society. By expanding the role of the judiciary as upper guardian, enhancing courts' ability to challenge discriminatory policies, and enacting comprehensive legislative changes, South Africa can move towards a legal framework that truly puts children first.

This approach requires a paradigm shift in how we view and implement laws and policies. It calls for courage from the judiciary to actively interpret the law in favour of children's interests and foresight from legislators to create a legal framework that prioritises the long-term well-being of the nation's youth.

Ultimately, by empowering these key institutions to champion the best interests of the child, we can create a society where every child, regardless of their background, has the opportunity to thrive and contribute to South Africa's future. This not only serves the interests of children but also lays the foundation for a more just, equitable, and prosperous nation for all.

14. A Vision for the Future

The best interests of the child principle offers a powerful path towards creating a more just and equitable society in South Africa. By prioritising this principle in all decision-making processes, we can address the root causes of inequality and discrimination that have persisted despite decades of redress efforts.

It was through enforcing my own constitutional rights in the children's courts, which continue to discriminate against fathers, that I realised the principle of the best interests of the child has the potential to challenge not only discrimination in children's courts but all discriminatory policies derived from the constitution, especially under the redress provision. While pursuing my own cause, I realised my struggle could help others, which is why I share it in my books. It's easy to feel despondent or give up in the face of South Africa's challenges, but we cannot afford to because these issues impact not only our present lives but also the future of our children.

Over the years, we have surrendered our authority and power as individuals to specialists, politicians, and other surrogates, believing they would act in our best interests. Now, we are paying the price, as our beautiful country is a shadow of its potential, with the born-free generation suffering the most. While specialists, politicians, and other surrogates have their place, it does not absolve us of our responsibility as individual citizens because we ultimately bear the cost of their decisions. It is important to realise that we all have the power to challenge any constitutional breach, thanks to the principle of equality before the law.

When we place children's welfare at the forefront, we naturally shift our focus from short-term political gains to long-term societal benefits. This approach encourages policies that invest in education, healthcare, and social support systems that benefit all children, regardless of their racial or socioeconomic background. By ensuring that every child has access to quality education and opportunities for personal growth, we lay the foundation for a more equitable society in the future.

Moreover, embracing the best interests of the child principle challenges us to move beyond the limitations of race-based policies. Instead of perpetuating divisions based on historical categories, we can focus on addressing the specific needs of each child. This individualised approach recognizes that children from all backgrounds may face unique challenges and ensures that support is provided based on need rather than demographic factors.

By prioritising children's interests, we also create a society that values potential over privilege. This shift can lead to a more meritocratic system where success is determined by individual ability and effort rather than inherited advantages or disadvantages. In turn, this can foster greater social mobility and reduce entrenched inequalities over time.

14.1. Call to Action

The path to a more equitable society begins with active citizenship. Every South African has the power and responsibility to challenge discriminatory laws and policies that undermine children's welfare. As outlined in "Goliath's Reckoning," tools like the Promotion of Access to Information Act (PAIA) provide accessible means for citizens to hold institutions accountable and advocate for change.

We call upon all citizens to:

- Educate themselves about children's rights and the best interests principle.
- Use PAIA and other legal tools to request information about policies affecting children.
- Engage with local representatives and policymakers to advocate for child-centric reforms.
- Support organisations working to protect children's rights and promote equality.

To policymakers and legal professionals, we urge a commitment to reforms that prioritise children's welfare and individual merit. This includes:

- Reviewing and amending existing laws to ensure they align with the best interests principle.
- Developing new policies focused on addressing children's needs rather than demographic quotas.
- Implementing training programs on children's rights and the best interests principle for all professionals working with children.
- Creating mechanisms for children's voices to be heard in policy-making processes.

For society as a whole, we encourage a shift in perspective that recognizes every child as a valuable member of our community, deserving of equal opportunities and protection. This involves:

- Challenging our own biases and preconceptions about race, gender, and social status.
- Fostering a culture of inclusivity and respect in our homes, schools, and communities.
- Supporting initiatives that promote cross-cultural understanding and cooperation among children.
- Valuing and nurturing the potential of every child, regardless of their background.

14.2. Key Points

Throughout this book, we have examined the complex interplay between South Africa's redress policies and the principle of the best interests of the child. We have argued that:

- The current approach to redress, while well-intentioned, has often perpetuated inequality and discrimination.

- The best interests of the child principle, as enshrined in the Constitution, offers a more effective framework for achieving true equity.
- All policies, even those not directly aimed at children, ultimately impact their lives and should be evaluated through this lens.
- A shift towards merit-based approaches and individual assessment can better serve children's needs than broad demographic categorizations.
- The judiciary, particularly the High Court as upper guardian, has a crucial role to play in upholding children's rights and challenging discriminatory practices.

14.3. The Road Ahead

As we look to the future, the importance of the best interests principle in shaping a fair and equitable South Africa cannot be overstated. This principle offers a unifying vision that transcends racial and political divides, focusing instead on our shared commitment to the next generation.

By consistently applying this principle, we can create a society where every child has the opportunity to reach their full potential. This not only serves the interests of individual children but also strengthens the fabric of our nation, fostering social cohesion, economic growth, and democratic stability.

The road ahead will not be easy. It requires us to confront uncomfortable truths about the limitations of our current approaches and to make difficult choices that may challenge entrenched interests. However, the potential rewards – a truly equitable society where every child can thrive – make this journey not just worthwhile, but essential.

14.4. Commitment to Change

As we conclude this exploration, we call for an ongoing commitment to reform discriminatory practices and promote the welfare of all children. This is not a task that can be completed overnight, nor is it the responsibility of any single group or institution. It requires sustained effort from all sectors of society – government, civil society, communities, and individuals.

We must remain vigilant in identifying and challenging practices that undermine children's interests, even when they come cloaked in the language of redress or equality. We must be willing to engage in difficult conversations about race, privilege, and opportunity, always keeping the welfare of children at the centre of these discussions.

Most importantly, we must never lose sight of the transformative power of prioritising children's interests. By committing to this principle, we invest not just in individual children, but in the future of our nation. Every child whose potential is nurtured, every young mind that is empowered, brings us one step closer to the just and equitable society we all aspire to create.

The choice before us is clear. We can continue down the path of division and demographic categorization, or we can embrace a future where every child is valued, protected, and given the opportunity to succeed. By choosing the latter, we honour the spirit of our Constitution and the dreams of those who fought for a free and equal South Africa. The journey towards this vision begins anew with each child, each decision, and each commitment we make to prioritise their best interests above all else.

Appendices

Glossary of Key Terms

- **Affirmative Action:** Policies that aim to increase the representation of historically disadvantaged groups in areas such as employment, education, and business.
- **Apartheid:** A system of institutionalised racial segregation and discrimination that existed in South Africa from 1948 to 1994.
- **Bantu Education Act:** A 1953 law that established a separate education system for black South Africans.
- **Best Interests of the Child:** The principle that the well-being and development of a child should be the primary consideration in all matters concerning them.
- **Black Economic Empowerment (BEE):** A policy aimed at increasing black ownership and participation in the South African economy.
- **Born-Frees:** The generation of South Africans born after apartheid ended in 1994.
- **Children's Act:** A comprehensive South African law that aims to protect children's rights and promote their well-being.
- **Children's Court:** A specialised court in South Africa that deals with matters concerning children.
- **Colonialism:** The policy or practice of acquiring full or partial political control over another country, occupying it with settlers, and exploiting it economically.
- **Constitution:** The supreme law of a country that establishes the framework for its government and defines the rights and responsibilities of its citizens.
- **Discrimination:** The unjust or prejudicial treatment of different categories of people, especially on the grounds of race, age, or sex.

- **Equality Before the Law:** The principle that all people are subject to the same laws and should be treated equally by the legal system.
- **Fair Discrimination:** A term used in the South African Constitution to allow for affirmative action measures that aim to redress past discrimination.
- **Family Advocate:** A legal professional appointed by the court to represent the best interests of a child in legal proceedings.
- **Gender-Based Violence (GBV):** Violence directed against a person because of their gender. It constitutes a breach of human rights and a form of discrimination.
- **The Homeschooling Father, Why and How I got Started:** A book by Salatiso that details his experiences and insights on homeschooling his children, challenging the traditional education system and advocating for parental empowerment in education.
- **Goliath's Reckoning:** A book by Salatiso that exposes the biassed truth behind the Children's Court and its discrimination against fathers.
- **Goliath's Stand:** A book by Salatiso that details his legal challenge against systemic discrimination in South Africa's Children's Courts.
- **High Court:** The superior court in South Africa that has jurisdiction over civil and criminal matters, and constitutional matters.
- **Maternal Preference Rule:** A legal principle that historically favoured mothers in child custody disputes.
- **Meritocracy:** A system where advancement is based on individual ability or achievement.
- **Migrant Labour System:** A system in which people leave their homes to work in another region or country.
- **National Development Plan (NDP):** A long-term strategic plan for South Africa's development.
- **Preferential Procurement:** A policy that gives preference to certain groups, such as black-owned businesses, in the awarding of government contracts.

- **Promotion of Access to Information Act (PAIA):** A South African law that gives people the right to access information held by public and private bodies.
- **Promotion of Administrative Justice Act (PAJA):** A South African law that promotes lawful, reasonable, and procedurally fair administrative action.
- **Rainbow Nation:** A term used to describe post-apartheid South Africa, emphasising its diverse population and the hope for unity and reconciliation.
- **Redress:** The act of setting right a wrong or injustice.
- **Section 28 of the Constitution:** The section of the South African Bill of Rights that enshrines children's rights.
- **Section 9 of the Constitution:** The section of the South African Bill of Rights that guarantees equality before the law and prohibits unfair discrimination.
- **Tender Years Doctrine:** A legal principle that historically favoured mothers in child custody disputes involving young children.
- **Ubuntu:** A Nguni Bantu term roughly translating to "humanity towards others." It is often used in a philosophical sense to mean "the belief in a universal bond of sharing that connects all humanity."
- **Unfair Discrimination:** Discrimination that is based on prohibited grounds, such as race, gender, or disability, and that cannot be justified as fair.
- **The Homeschooling Father:** A book by Salatiso that details his experiences and insights on homeschooling his child.
- **Unravelling Xhosa History:** A book by Salatiso that explores the history and culture of the Xhosa people.

Case Summaries

- **AB and Another v Minister of Social Development (2016):** This case challenged the constitutionality of a law requiring a genetic link in surrogacy agreements. The Constitutional Court upheld the law but acknowledged the discriminatory impact on individuals unable to contribute a gamete.

- **Centre for Child Law v Minister of Social Development (2009):** This case successfully challenged discriminatory provisions in the Children's Act that disadvantaged children born out of wedlock.
- **FS v JJ and Others (2011):** This case established the best interests of the child as the primary consideration in relocation disputes, emphasising the need to consider a wide range of factors affecting the child's well-being.
- **JT v Road Accident Fund (2015):** This case affirmed that the best interests of the child should be paramount in determining damages awarded in personal injury claims, considering the child's future needs.
- **S v M (2008):** This case highlighted the importance of considering the best interests of the child in sentencing decisions, particularly when the offender is a primary caregiver.

Legislative Texts

- **Section 28 of the Constitution of the Republic of South Africa, 1996:** This section enshrines the rights of children, including the right to family care, basic nutrition, healthcare, and protection from maltreatment, neglect, abuse, and exploitation. It also establishes the principle that the best interests of the child are of paramount importance in every matter concerning the child.
- **Section 9 of the Constitution of the Republic of South Africa, 1996:** This section guarantees equality before the law and prohibits unfair discrimination on various grounds, including race, gender, sex, pregnancy, marital status, ethnic or social origin, colour, sexual orientation, age, disability, religion, conscience, belief, culture, language, and birth.
- **The Children's Act 38 of 2005:** This comprehensive legislation provides a framework for protecting children's rights and promoting their well-being. It covers various aspects of child welfare, including

parental rights and responsibilities, child protection, adoption, foster care, and the administration of children's estates.

Bibliography

- Allen, "Surrogacy, Slavery, and the Ownership of Life" (1990) 139 *Harvard Journal of Law and Public Policy* 144
- Banda, "Building on a global movement: Violence against women in the African context" (2008) 8 *African Human Rights Law Journal* 1
- Barrett and Burman, "Deciding the best interests of the child: an international perspective on custody decision-making" (2001) 118 *SALJ* 556
- Bato Star Fishing (Pty) Ltd v Minister of Environmental Affairs and Tourism [2004] ZACC 15; 2004 (4) SA 490 (CC); 2004 (7) BCLR 687 (CC)
- Bekker, *Seymour's Customary Law in Southern Africa* 5 ed (Juta & Co Limited, Cape Town 1989)
- Belo v Commissioner of Child Welfare, Johannesburg, and Others: Belo v Chapelle and Another [2002] 3 All SA 286 (W)
- Benatar, *Better Never to Have Been: The Harm of Coming into Existence* (Oxford University Press, New York 2006)
- Bennett, "The best interests of the child in an African context" (1999) 20 *Obiter* 145
- Bernstein v Bester NO [1996] ZACC 2; 1996 (2) SA 751 (CC); 1996 (4) BCLR 449 (CC)
- Bhulwana; S v Gwadiso [1995] ZACC 11; 1996 (1) SA 388 (CC); 1995 (12) BCLR 1579 (CC)
- Biowatch Trust v Registrar Genetic Resources [2009] ZACC 14; 2009 (6) 232 (CC); 2009 (10) BCLR 1014 (CC)
- Bishop and Woolman, "Freedom and Security of the Person" in Woolman et al (eds) 2 ed (Juta & Co Limited, Cape Town 2012)
- Brandt v S [2005] 2 All SA 1 (SCA)

• Brown et al, "Reframing the Debate around State Responses to Infertility: Considering the Harms of Subfertility and Involuntary Childlessness" (2016) *Public Health Ethics* 1

• Burchell and Milton, *Principles of Criminal Law* 3 ed (Juta, Landsdowne 2005)

• Bush, *Spoken from the Heart* (Simon & Schuster, New York 2010)

• Carmichele v Minister of Safety and Security [2001] ZACC 22; 2001 (4) SA 938 (CC); 2001 (10) BCLR 995 (CC)

• *Certification of the Constitution of the Republic of South Africa, 1996* [1996] ZACC 26; 1996 (4) SA 744 (CC); 1996 (10) BCLR 1253 (CC)

• City Council of Pretoria v Walker [1998] ZACC 1; 1998 (2) SA 363 (CC); 1998 (3) BCLR 257 (CC)

• Coetzee v Government of the Republic of South Africa; Matiso v Commanding Officer, Port Elizabeth Prison [1995] ZACC 7; 1995 (4) SA 631 (CC); 1995 (10) BCLR 1382 (CC)

• *Constitution of the Republic of South Africa*, 1996

• Cool Ideas 1186 CC v Hubbard [2014] ZACC 16; 2014 (4) SA 474 (CC); 2014 (8) BCLR 869 (CC)

• Cowden, "'No Harm, No Foul': A Child's Right to Know their Genetic Parents" (2012) 26(1) *International Journal of Law, Policy and the Family* 102

• Currie and de Waal, *The Bill of Rights Handbook* 6 ed (Juta, Cape Town 2013)

• Daar, "Accessing Reproductive Technologies: Invisible Barriers, Indelible Harms" (2013) 23 *Berkeley Journal of Gender, Law & Justice* 30

• De Lange v Smuts NO [1998] ZACC 6; 1998 (3) SA 785 (CC); 1998 (7) BCLR 779 (CC)

• De Reuck v Director of Public Prosecutions (Witwatersrand Local Division) [2003] ZACC 19; 2004 (1) SA 406 (CC); 2003 (12) BCLR 1333 (CC)

- Dikoko v Mokhatla [2006] ZACC 10; 2006 (6) SA 235 (CC); 2007 (1) BCLR 1 (CC)
- Director of Public Prosecutions, KwaZulu-Natal v P 2006 (3) SA 515 (SCA); [2006] 1 All SA 446 (SCA); 2006 (1) SACR 243 (SCA)
- Domar et al, "The Prevalence and Predictability of Depression in Infertile Women" (1992) 58 *Fertility and Sterility* 1158
- Dworkin, *The Theory and Practice of Autonomy* (Cambridge University Press, Cambridge 1988)
- Dyer et al, "'Men leave me as I cannot have children': Women's experiences with involuntary childlessness" (2002) 17 *Human Reproduction* 1663
- Dyer et al, "'You are a man because you have children': Experiences, reproductive health knowledge and treatment-seeking behaviour among men suffering from couple infertility in South Africa" (2004) 19 *Human Reproduction* 960
- Els E v Bruce; Els J v Bruce 1922 EDL 295
- Ermelo at para 70
- Fenton-Glynn, Claire. "Human Rights and Private International Law: Regulating International Surrogacy" (2014) 10 *Journal of Private International Law* 157
- Ferreira v Levin NO; Vryenhoek v Powell NO [1995] ZACC 13; 1996 (1) SA 984 (CC); 1996 (1) BCLR 1 (CC)
- *Firearms Control Act* 60 of 2000
- Fletcher v Fletcher 1948 (1) SA 130 (A)
- Fourie [2005] ZACC 19; 2006 (1) SA 524 (CC); 2006 (3) BCLR 355 (CC)
- Freeman et al, "Psychological Evaluation and Support in a Program of In Vitro Fertilisation and Embryo Transfer" (1985) 43 *Fertility & Sterility* 48
- Frith, "Gamete donation and anonymity: The ethical legal debate" (2001) 16 *Human Reproduction* 821

- Goliath's Reckoning: Unveiling the Biassed Truth Behind Children's Court that discriminates against Fathers by Salatiso Mdeni
- Goliath's Stand: Challenging Discrimination in the Equality Court – A Fight Against Systemic Discrimination in South Africa's Children's Courts by Salatiso Mdeni
- Pinker, S. (2002). The Blank Slate: The Modern Denial of Human Nature. New York: Viking.
- Government of the Republic of South Africa and Others v Grootboom and Others 2001 (1) SA 46 (CC); 2000 (11) BCLR 1169 (CC)
- Govender 1995 (1) SACR 492 (N)
- H v Fetal Assessment Centre [2014] ZACC 34; 2015 (2) SA 193 (CC); 2015 (2) BCLR 127 (CC)
- Harksen v Lane NO [1997] ZACC 12; 1998 (1) SA 300 (CC); 1997 (11) BCLR 1489 (CC)
- Head of Department, Department of Education, Free State Province v Welkom High School; Head of Department, Department of Education, Free State Province v Harmony High School [2013] ZACC 25; 2014 (2) SA 228 (CC); 2013 (9) BCLR
- Democratic Republic of the Congo: Cobalt Mining and Child Labor. Amnesty International. Retrieved from https://www.amnesty.org/en/latest/news/2016/01/child-labour-behind-smart-phone-and-electric-car-batteries/
- Cobalt Mining in Congo: Child Labor and the Supply Chain. Human Rights Watch. Retrieved from https://www.hrw.org/report/2020/11/18/child-labor-cobalt-mines/congo
- Burkina Faso and Mali: Child Labor in Gold Mining. International Labour Organization (ILO). Retrieved from https://www.ilo.org/global/topics/child-labour/lang—en/index.htm
- Child Labor in Gold Mining: Health Risks and Educational Impact. UNICEF. Retrieved from https://www.unicef.org/reports/child-labor-mining

● Cocoa Farming and Child Labor in Côte d'Ivoire and Ghana. U.S. Department of Labor. Retrieved from https://www.dol.gov/agencies/ilab/reports/child-labor/cocoa

● Exploitation of Child Labor in Cocoa Plantations. International Cocoa Initiative. Retrieved from https://www.cocoainitiative.org/news

● Child Labor on Tea Plantations in Kenya. Kenya Human Rights Commission. Retrieved from https://www.khrc.or.ke/publications.html

● Child Labor in Kenya's Tea Industry. Save the Children. Retrieved from https://www.savethechildren.org/us/about-us/resource-library

www.ingramcontent.com/pod-product-compliance
Lightning Source LLC
LaVergne TN
LVHW090426210926
848480LV00002B/707
* 9 7 9 8 2 3 1 7 6 9 6 7 4 *